12 Days to the Rescue!
TRIM the TREE at CHRISTMAS

By Christine Berg

Truly Unique Gifting

Welcome to Christmas gifting made fun! This book gives you all the assistance you need to put together unforgettable presents for everyone in your life. Whether you would like to provide group presents for multiple families or give a single person a special gift, this guide takes away all the guesswork and leaves you giving a truly distinctive gift that will be loved by all!

Other Books in this Series:

A Colorful Christmas

Christmas Around the World

A Partridge in a Pear Tree Christmas

Caroling Through Christmas

www.12daystotherescue.com

Cover design by Ember & Co Design Studio

12 Days to the Rescue
Trim the Tree at Christmas

Christine Berg
Cover design by Ember & Co Design Studio

ISBN: 978-1-7328150-0-1

To Karl

Who always believed

Even, especially, when I doubted

Would not have happened without you

INTRODUCTION

I am not a good gifter. I try, I really do, but that clever, thoughtful, just-right something that will be loved and cherished forever (or thoroughly enjoyed in the moment) usually escapes me. I did it once: the year I got my Dad a leather tool-belt. He didn't ask for it, but I could tell when he opened the present that it completely hit the mark and he really loved it. So, I know the feeling- that wonderful satisfaction of pleasing your givee. But because that rarely happened, Christmas shopping for me was agony. I am not overstating. Even after my budget allowed a wider range of choices, finding that elusive "perfect gift" for siblings, grandparents, parents and in-laws was pressure filled and painful. If you can relate, then *12 Days to the Rescue* is for you! It will literally rescue you from suffering and distress. (OK- maybe a little overstating). This book follows a theme of gifts for 12 days starting with Christmas that can be customized for everyone on your shopping list. There are options given for different ages, individuals, families and monetary amounts. I give you the tags and ideas for wrapping. You can do as much or little as you like with this. People <u>love</u> these! So, with the stressful question of, "What do I get them?" taken care of, you can relax knowing you are giving a great gift and actually enjoy the rest of the holiday season. You will become an awesome gifter and finally it truly will be better to give than to receive.

Twelve days of gifts?! That might seem a lot harder and costlier than one nice gift per person. If you can do that- find what you want on the web, click a few times and have your gift magically sent off to give Christmas spirit- go for it! I highly recommend it. However, if scrolling through hundreds of items online or scouring aisles in stores to find what you want, or even to know what you want, leaves you glassy-eyed and feeling frustrated, this book is a real de-stressor. This works especially well when gifting many families. And, when you buy in bulk and split apart, it really does get less expensive. Now let's get started!

Tips:
- First things first: Establish a budget- either per person or per household. Divide by 12 for your allotted amount per gift day. Obviously if you spend less on one day, you can allocate that to spend a little more an another.
- The earlier in the year you begin, the more you can watch for sales!
- Buy in bulk and split up whenever possible.
- If you are a baker, gifts of mixes or baked treats are great fun and stretch easily for several recipients.
- Often one gift can serve a whole family.
- When ordering items online, give yourself time for things to be delivered to you before you need to send them on. If you are mailing your 12 Days to the Rescue gifts, remember the post office deadlines.
- Collecting fun things to give away does take up space; you may want to dedicate a couple of shelves in a closet to keep everything sorted and stored.
- *Please personalize this as much as possible!* I am only giving suggestions, you know the tastes of those you are gifting the best!

Trim the Tree!

Our gifting theme remembers an old German tradition of 12 ornaments that represent 12 qualities of a happy home. Each day's gift will be centered around one of these. Since this theme is generated by ornaments, you can include the appropriate one as a gift decoration, or the gift itself. Or, use the gift tags provided (at the end of the book) as ornaments, particularly if you choose to embellish them. The pictures provide enhancement suggestions for the crafty among you!

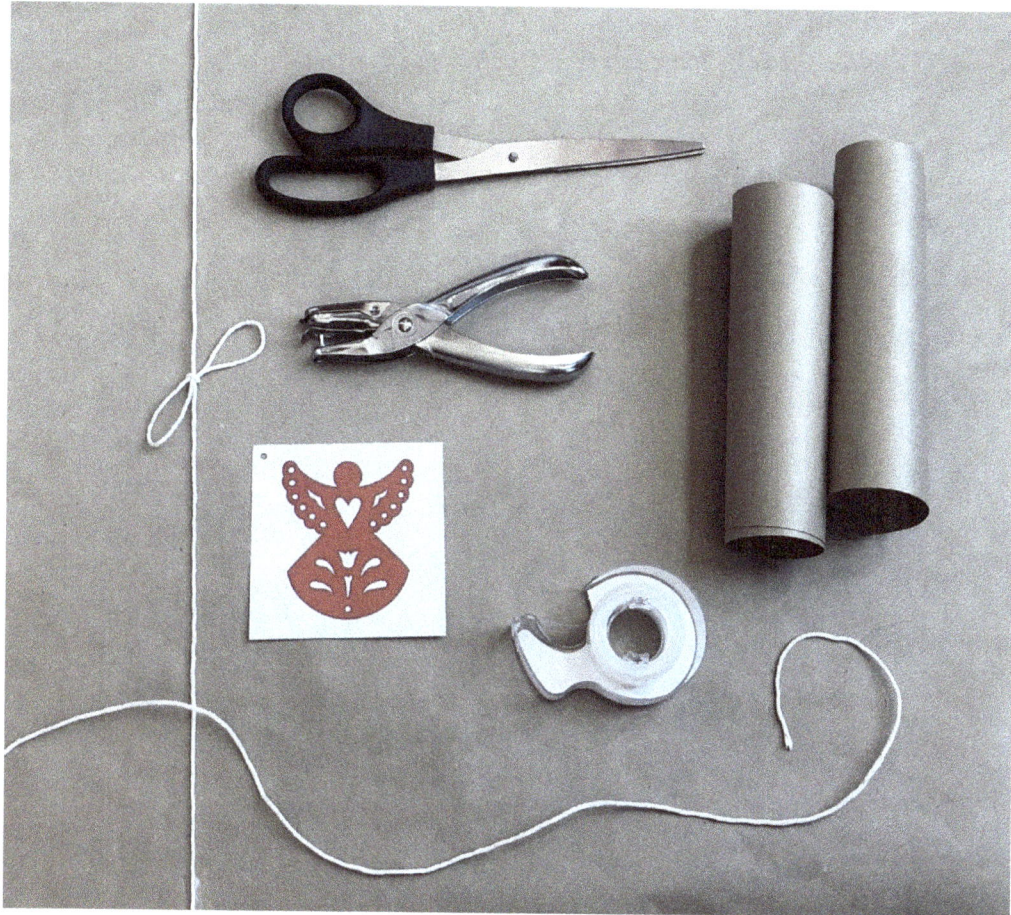

Wrapping recommendation: Since this theme has an "Old World" feel, keep the mood by wrapping your gifts in brown paper and use white kite string as ribbon. A bit of greenery and the gift tags will add a splash of Christmassy fun!

MERRY CHRISTMAS!

The very first thing your giftees will open is a card that carries the explanation of what you are giving this year. You need only one per giving group. (i.e. only one for your sister, her husband and kids, but also one for your grandmother, who lives alone). This truly piques excitement! Opening a present starts on Christmas Day, so if your tradition is celebrating Christmas Eve, on that night they open the card only. If you celebrate on Christmas Day, they would open the card along with the first day's gift. On the gift tag, write a personal note for that special touch!

The First Day of Christmas: December 25

The first ornament of our twelve days of gifting is a FRUIT BASKET. At this time of year where much of the country is in hibernation, think of a bowl overflowing with all varieties of exotic fruits. The picture is abundance, from which we share with others. "Generosity" is the quality it represents.

Gift Ideas: (mix & match, pick & choose)
- For **Couples** or **Families**: Actually, for all categories: give anything fruit related, even the dreaded fruit-cake for those that like it. A stollen is very tasty and travels well. Favorite jams and jellies would be a nice gift here- particularly if you make them yourself! A box of exotic fruit is a classic Christmas gift.
- For **Adults**: Try apple cider mix either from the store or home-made along with a gallon of real cider. Or better yet, mulling spices. Of course, any of the food items from the above category work as well. Another thought would be to give gift wrapping sets for them to use when being generous and giving to others.
- For **Teens**: They might like a Fruit-of-the-Loom hoodie or other active wear items or T-shirts. Or, how about a gift card to a juice bar?
- For **Kids**: Fruit snacks would be a big hit and there are many healthy options to choose from.

The Second Day of Christmas: December 26

Coming into a warm, cozy home from the blistering cold must be the thought behind the second ornament. It is a HOUSE and it represents "Protection and Safety." I love the idea that at home, among family and friends, we can be sheltered not only from the physical elements, but also from hurts and struggles of the outside world. My hope is that each of you have such a refuge.

Gift Ideas: (mix & match, pick & choose)
- For **Couples** or **Families**: Your recipes handed down from generations that shine at potlucks make great gifts. For a kit, put together all the non-perishables along with a recipe card that states, "From our House to Yours." Another idea is to give a needed household item that all would enjoy.
- For **Adults**: Since the meaning is one of protection, you can go the route of safety: first aid kits, passport or credit card protection sleeves. Or, for protection from the elements- a fun umbrella.
- For **Teens:** Any of the ideas for adults would be great for teens as well: car safety kit, passport or credit card protection sleeves, umbrella. You can go the "House" route and get them something fun for their room.
- For **Kids:** Try a headlight or reflective material for hiking or biking at night, or an ID bracelet. If you go the "house" angle you can pick out something for their bedroom like a pillow or bulletin board. For the ultimate Christmas "house" gift, send along a gingerbread house kit.

The Third Day of Christmas: December 27

The third ornament is a FISH. Yes, whoever started this whole tradition decided that a fish would be a desirable bauble on any self-respecting Christmas tree. It means to represent "Blessings on the Home." That, of course, *is* sought-after and we will go with it!

Gift Ideas: (mix & match, pick & choose)
- For **Everyone:** Christmas started with the birth of Christ, and a fish is a popular Christian symbol. It is found on jewelry, journals, mugs, pens and more.
- For **Couples** or whole **Families**: Give a Fish Fry mix (homemade or from the store) or any cooking or grilling equipment. You can give a fish-related movie (Finding Nemo, Moby Dick, etc.). A gift card to a seafood restaurant would be a great treat.
- For **Adults**: If they fish, you are in luck! A new fishing lure, other fishing equipment or a gift card to a sporting goods store would work well. If there are no fishermen, send along smoked fish & crackers. Or, use any of the gift ideas mentioned above.
- For **Teens**: Again, if they fish, or are able to try, fishing equipment. If not, one of the classic thriller movies about sharks or whales would be good. After checking with parents, a real goldfish might be fun. For fashionistas, try a trendy fishing hat.
- For **Kids**: Children will always be the easiest people to shop for. Anything with a fish on it will do: fishing video game, fish stickers, fish book, fish T-shirt, fish crackers, etc.

The Fourth Day of Christmas: December 28

Our ornament for the fourth day of Christmas is a PINE CONE. The old legend says that it represents "Fruitfulness." Let's see if we can't have some fun with this one, too!

Gift Ideas: (mix & match, pick & choose)

- For **Couples** and **Families**: At this time of year, there are all sorts of seasonal decorations made with pine cones. Find something you think your friends and families will like that stays within your budget. A family activity gift would be to give pine cones, a jar of peanut butter, a plastic bag of bird seed and some ribbon. Give the simple instructions: roll the pine cones in peanut butter and then roll them in birdseed. Finally, attach a ribbon to hang on a tree outside for the birds and squirrels.

- For **Adults**: This one is a toughie for men. Women love the decorations. For guys- and gals- we'll take the Pinecone theme to the woods! A nice scarf, hat or warm gloves would be just the thing for a hike among the fir trees. You can also give any item that has a pinecone or fir tree as a decoration- travel mug, hand towels, etc.

- For **Teens**: A travel mug or graphic T with a pinecone or fir tree on it is a good start for teenagers. Or if your teen drives a car or plays a sport, a pine-scented freshener might be just the thing. Gloves, mittens, hats or scarves would be good for this gift as well.

- For **Kids**: Children would enjoy making the above treat for the animals outside. And you can give them a fun hat to wear while they pick the perfect spot to hang their creation.

The Fifth Day of Christmas: December 29

Good old SAINT NICOLAUS makes an appearance in our 12 Days of Christmas! He represents "Goodwill" which is very appropriate considering who he was historically as well as the jolly contemporary version he is today.

Gift Ideas: (mix & match, pick & choose)
- For **Everyone:** Give note-cards. Determine the style and number to match your giftees. These are meant for everyone to write at least one note of encouragement to someone who might need it this season. Young children can draw a picture on theirs. You might also want to include Santa hats for everyone. They can wear them while writing their notes and make a party of it!
- You can also give a paper bag for them to fill with gently-used items no longer wanted to take to a charity drop-off, to spread Goodwill to others. If you go with them and get a treat afterwards, you will have created a memory, too.

The Sixth Day of Christmas: December 30

Today's ornament is a ROSE. This might be a bit of a surprise considering the time of year. Maybe that's the point! The thought of lovely roses warms the heart particularly when the outdoors is a frozen landscape. It is no surprise that it signifies "Beauty & Affection." And what better time of year for friendship and hugs!

Gift Ideas: (mix & match, pick & choose)
- For **Families, Couples & Adults**: Give a mirror (that goes with their décor) with a note that says, "You are a work of art!" Or maybe a gift that literally says, "I love you" like a mug, or wall hanging, or piece of jewelry. Chocolate roses are a tasty add-on to the gift.
- For **Teens**: Some girls would like a mirror. Or anything that has a rose on it (mug, picture frame, pillow). For others and the guys, you need to go more toward the affection route with a mug or plaque that tells them how great they are. (I.e. "World's Best ____"; or "I/we heart you".) If there is a creative interest, give an artist kit so they can make their own something beautiful.
- For **Kids**: Girly girls would love anything with a rose like coloring books, tea sets, or stickers. Boys and girls enjoy art kits- there are many different kinds available that cover a wide range of interests. And I know I don't have to remind you about the chocolate roses for the kids!

The Seventh Day of Christmas: December 31
New Year's Eve!

As love is the heart of every home, it is fitting that the next ornament is a HEART and of course, it represents "Love." As this year comes to a close, take a moment to consider not only those you love, but also all the love you have received.

Gift Idea:
- For **Everyone**: Either give as one gift for all, or one per person: Find a suitable picture frame with a picture of yourself (include everyone that is giving this gift) with a note that says, " We/ I love you!"

The Eighth Day of Christmas: January 1
New Year's Day!

Here we have another unconventional ornament: a RABBIT. It is understood to represent "Hope." Why not?! It seems fitting for this day. As we embark on a new year, take a moment to consider what you might hope for.

Gift Ideas: (mix & match, pick & choose)
- For **Families:** This gift can be all about the rabbit. Carrot cake or carrot muffins (or mixes) are great for groups.
- For **Couples, Adults** and **Teens:** The calorie-conscious might enjoy a gourmet rabbit-food (salad) topping mix. Or a gift card to a restaurant known for great salads. Or, go with the carrot cake!
- For **Kids:** Give them a stuffed rabbit or a classic children's book that has rabbits, such as, Robert Munsch's *I'll Love You Forever* for youngest ones or *Watership Down* by Richard Adams for those a little older.

The Ninth Day of Christmas: January 2

This day's gift is centered on the classic Christmas symbol, an ANGEL. Here the angel represents "Guidance." Life is a journey, and we can't go it alone. We all need some guidance along the way.

Gift Ideas: (mix & match, pick & choose)
- For **Everyone:** Even though smart phones are edging them out, maps are a great guide, quite fascinating and some are truly beautiful. They come in puzzles, on mugs, pillows, coasters, jewelry and phone cases. There are collector's maps for things like quarters and bottle caps. Do an online search and see what turns up. Have fun with this one- and don't forget to include a bag of trail mix for the journey!

Other ideas:
- For **Families**: An aerial map of where the family lives is a unique and personal gift. If the family travels at all, give a map of the United States or the World, where they can have fun filling in places they've been. Or you can go the angel route and give them an angel hair pasta kit with sauce for all to enjoy.
- For **Couples & Adults**: Add to the above ideas a quality travel journal. Or some might like an angel decoration.
- For **Teens**: A travel scrapbook kit would be a big hit. There are several guide books that can be fun. Any "how-to" guidebook or kit that shares their interest would be much appreciated.
- For **Kids**: A compass might just spark a lifetime enjoyment of orienteering. Or how about a National Parks passport book? Any child version of the family ideas would be perfect.

The Tenth Day of Christmas: January 3

A BIRD is the ornament of choice for this day. A red cardinal on a snowy fir tree is about as Christmassy as you can get! It really does proclaim what it is meant to represent: "Joy and Happiness."

Gift Ideas: (mix & match, pick & choose)
- For **Families**: You can go the early bird route: a gourmet pancake mix, gourmet syrups, or a gift card to a local restaurant that serves a nice breakfast/brunch.
- For **Couples** & **Adults**: Here you can really focus on the early bird with coffees, teas and creamers; anything early morning.
- For **Teens**: A gift card to the local coffee shop would be perfect.
- For **Kids**: Since the early bird gets the worm: gummy worms!

Of course, for all categories you can get them something- anything- that would bring them happiness and joy.

The Eleventh Day of Christmas: January 4

Flowers always bring a smile- which is the intention when they are a gift! The eleventh day's ornament is a FLOWER BASKET. It represents "Good Wishes," to make someone's day.

Gift Ideas: (mix & match, pick & choose)
- For **Families & Adults:** A terrarium kit (that includes flowers) would make a great gift for families and adults alike. Putting together a mini-world and then watching it grow is a gift that lasts all year long. If there are gardeners in the mix, give a packet of seeds and some garden tools. A poinsettia plant – the Christmas Flower- is also a very appropriate gift.
- For **Teens:** Mini terrariums with succulents lend an alien feel and would be great for teens. Here, again, anything with flowers on it would be great for young ladies.
- For **Kids:** Even children can put together their own mini-world with some help from parents. If that is too ambitious, they can have their own plant to care for and watch grow. You can also give them pennies and take a trip where there is a fountain to make a wish.

Be sure to greet everyone you meet with a smile!

The Twelfth Day of Christmas: January 5

For eleven days now your giftees have had fun discovering how your gift might relate to the theme of the day. This last day is no different. "Hospitality" is represented by today's ornament, a TEAPOT. Hospitality is where you create a safe place for others to be themselves. Serving tea and cookies conjures up this very idea. Any time is a good time to invite friends and have some fun being welcoming!

Gift Ideas: (mix & match, pick & choose)
- For **Families, Couples** and **Adults**: Give a gift that is meant to be shared. Something that would be great to practice hospitality with: party dip mix, a basket of cheese and crackers, include some nice desserts. If you have a signature cookie, make a batch for them to share. And, of course, you can give all things tea related: specialty teas, a beautiful teapot, fun mugs, or even coasters. Or, how about a welcome mat for their front door?
- For **Teens**: Again, gifts to share. Bags of chips and salsa, cookies, or whatever the favorite junk food trend is.
- For **Kids**: Young children can also participate in hospitality. Perhaps give them their favorite cookies to share with friends.

Finishing Touches: Gift Tags

For your gift tags, print off the following. Glossy brochure paper works well. Print out the words as well on either the same paper or simply use copy paper. Cut out the tags, fold them in half. Cut out the word squares and glue or tape them inside the corresponding tag. Don't forget to add your personal note! That is all you need to do. However, you can embellish the gift with some green picks, or even the ornament of the day. I gave a few examples of fun things to do with the tags throughout the book. I hope you have fun with them!

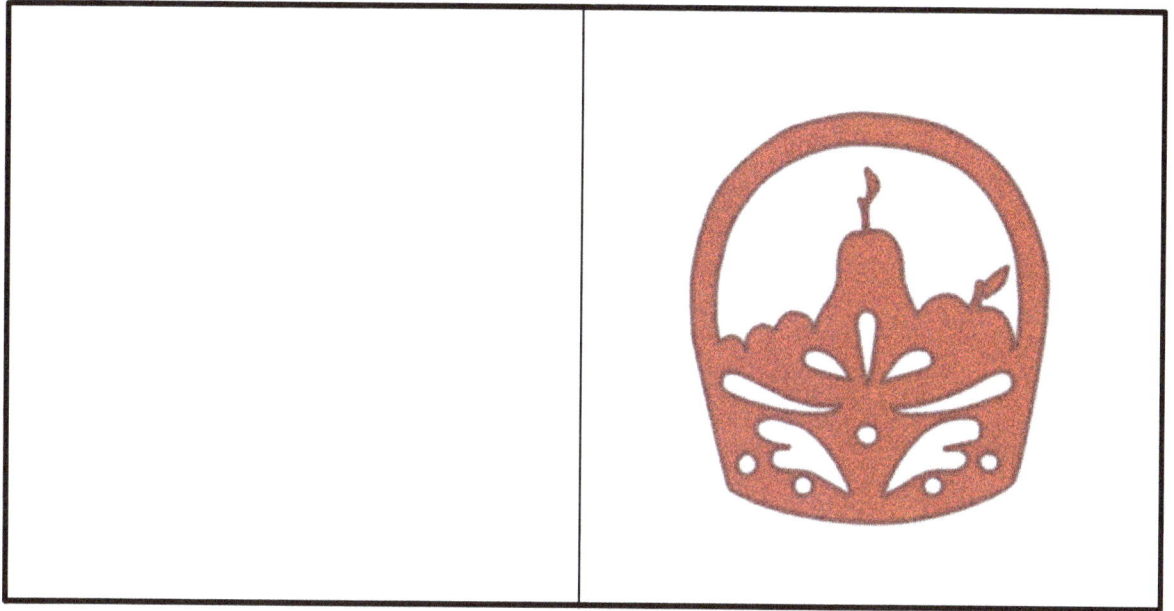

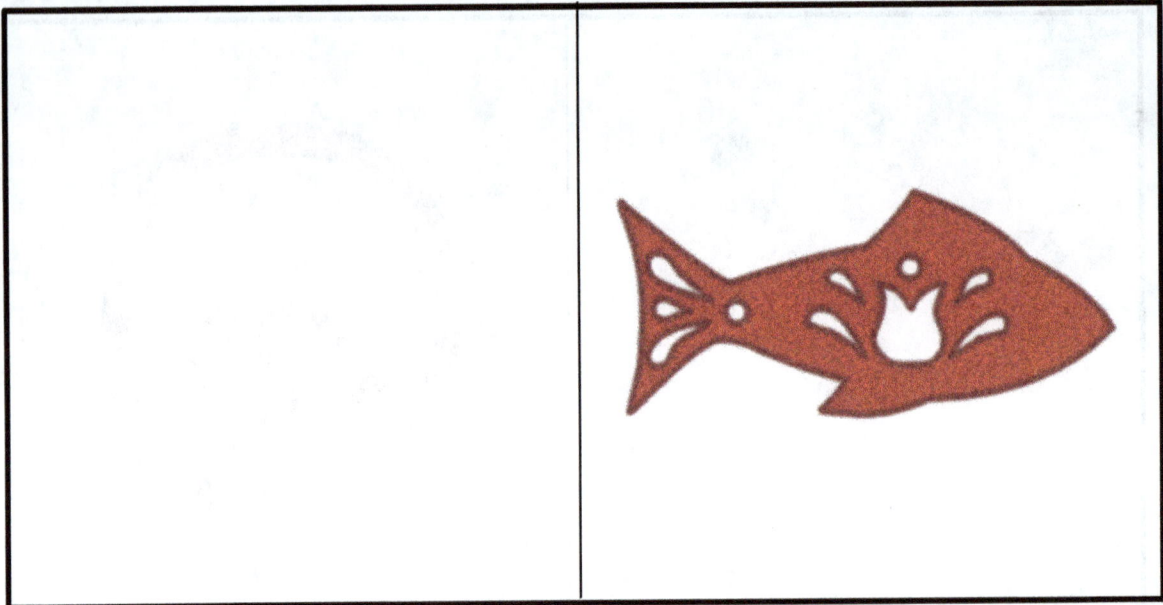

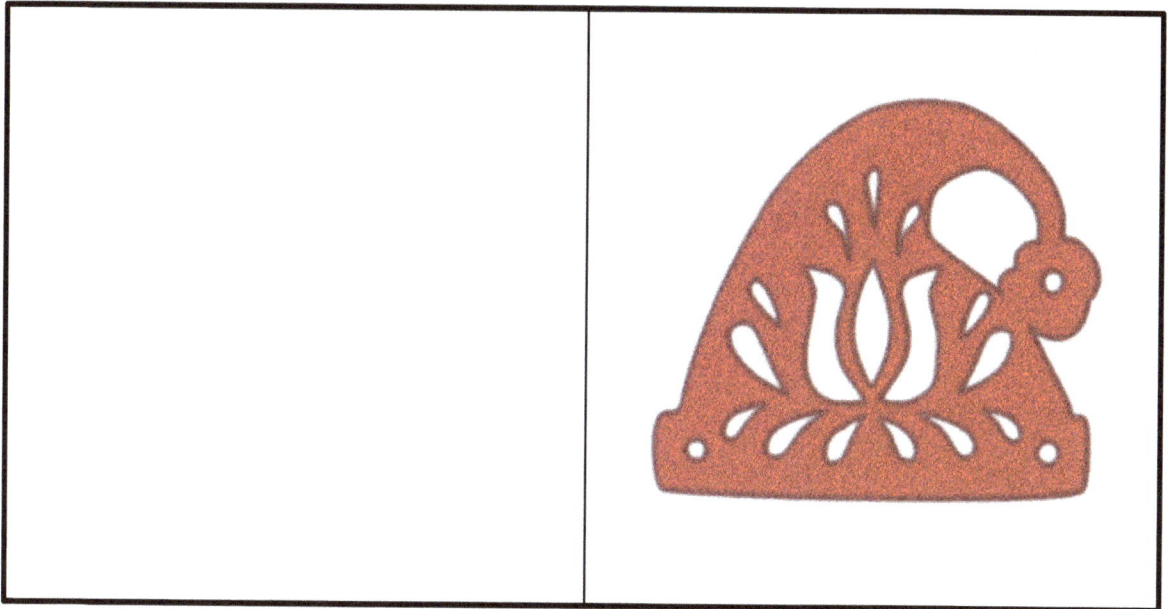

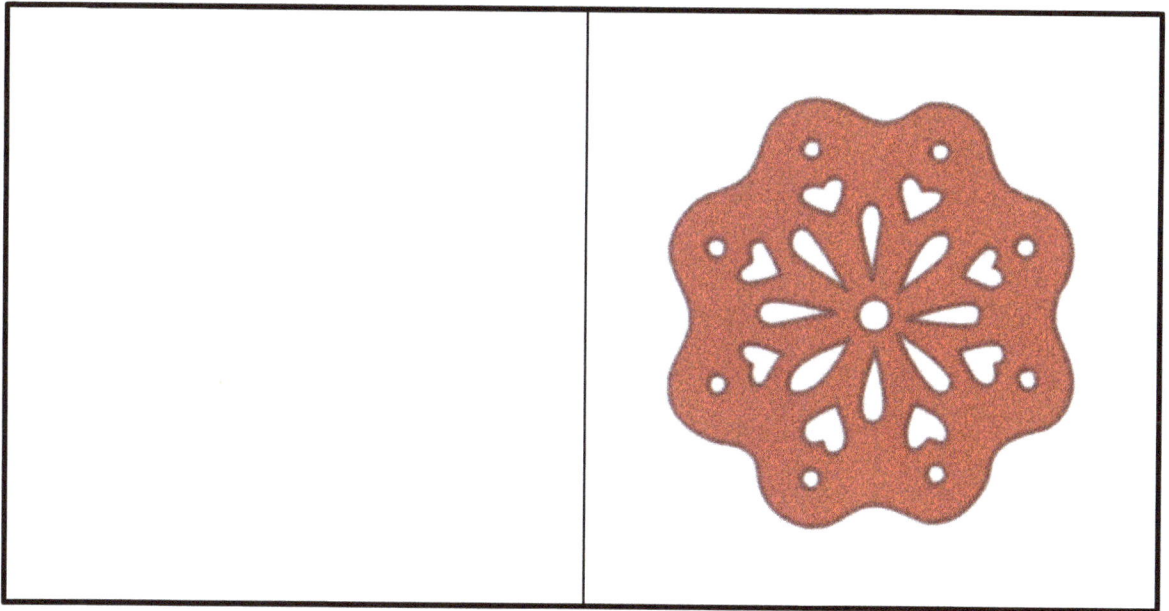

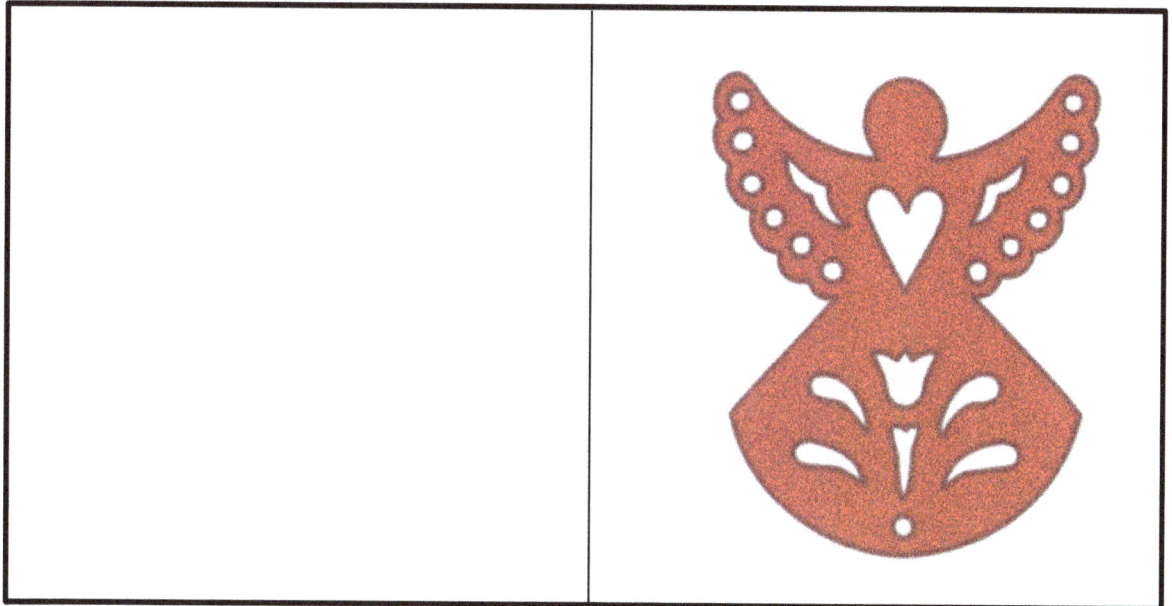

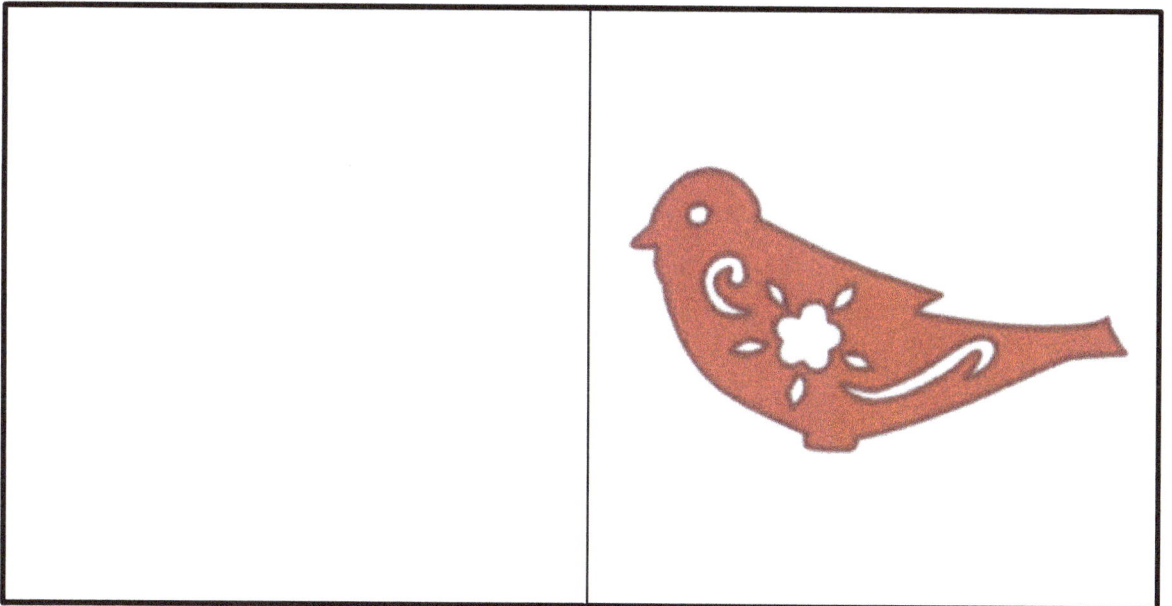

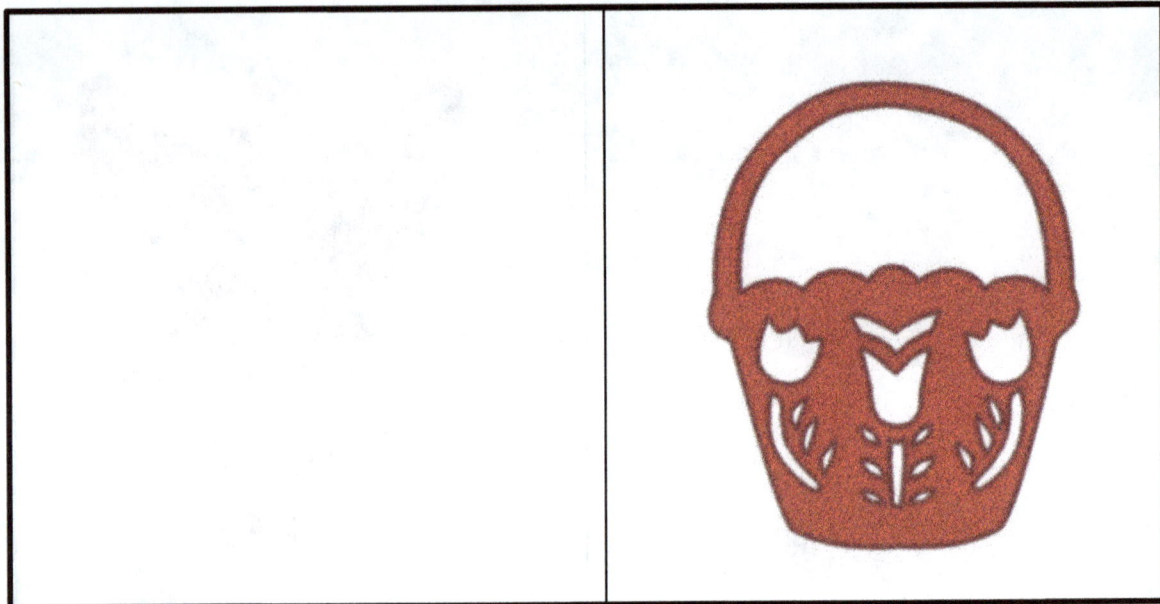

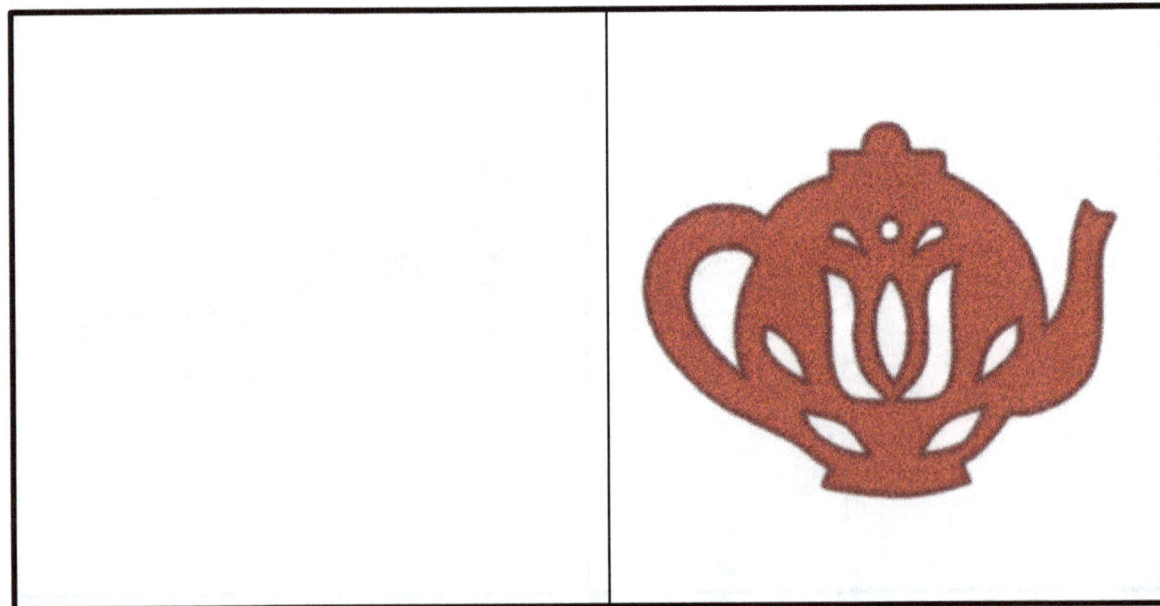

Inside Words:

You can simply write these words (or use your own) inside the corresponding tag above, or you can make copies, cut them out and tape or glue them inside the gift tags.

Merry Christmas!

Your gift this year is 12 Days of Christmas based loosely on an old German tradition of ornaments representing twelve things that everyone should have. Open each gift on its labeled day.

CHEERS!

December 25
The First Day of Christmas

A FRUIT BASKET is the first ornament in this tradition, representing the quality of "Generosity."

May the spirit of generosity extend through you to others!

December 26
The Second Day of Christmas

Coming into a warm and cozy home from the blistering cold must be the thought behind the second day's ornament: a HOUSE. It signifies "Protection and Safety."

December 27
The Third Day of Christmas

The next ornament is a FISH. It is meant to represent "Blessings on the Home."

Here is a fish-related blessing for you!

December 28
The Fourth Day of Christmas

"Fruitfulness" is the trait characterized in today's ornament, a PINE CONE.

Enjoy this fruit inspired treat!

December 29
The Fifth Day of Christmas

SAINT NICOLAUS makes an appearance! As with his legend, he embodies "Goodwill."

Here is something to help you spread goodwill to others.

December 30
The Sixth Day of Christmas

The sixth ornament in this tradition is a ROSE. It signifies "Beauty & Affection." A rose in winter truly is a lovely thing. And what better time for friendship and hugs!

December 31
The Seventh Day of Christmas

New Year's Eve is an appropriate day to think about today's quality, "Love," characterized by a HEART.

Take a moment to remember loved ones from this past year.

January 1
The Eighth Day of Christmas

Today's ornament is a RABBIT representing "Hope."

As we embark on a New Year, what do you hope for?

January 2
The Ninth Day of Christmas

"Guidance" is today's quality characterized by an ANGEL.

Life is a journey- we can't go it alone. We all need some guidance along the way.

January 3
The Tenth Day of Christmas

Seeing a BIRD on a snowy fir tree is about as Christmassy as you can get! It really does say what it means, "Joy and Happiness."

Here is something to make you happy!

January 4
The Eleventh Day of Christmas

The eleventh ornament is a FLOWER BASKET. Flowers always bring a smile, as they are meant to signify "Good Wishes."

Be sure to greet everyone you meet today with a smile!

January 5
The Twelfth Day of Christmas

The last ornament in this tradition is a TEAPOT. Serving tea and cookies summons the very idea behind it: "Hospitality."

Any time is a good time to invite friends and have some fun being welcoming!

I hope you have as much fun putting these gifts together as I do! I know your recipients are going to love them. Now relax, have a glass of eggnog and enjoy the holidays. Cheers!

About the Author:

Christine Berg loves all things Christmas: the food, the traditions, the decorations. However, her favorite part is the gathering of family and friends, especially the ever-expanding families of her four adult children. She and her husband enjoy hosting in their Colorado home and cherish multi-generations and people of various cultural backgrounds laughing and celebrating together. All things Christmas can be a lot of work, though, and this book hopes to ease the burden. Visit her website for other books in this series: 12daystotherescue.com.

12 Days to the Rescue